COLORS & MARKINGS OF THE
U.S. NAVY
F-4 PHANTOM

in detail & scale

Bert Kinzey & Ray Leader

KALMBACH BOOKS

Airlife Publishing Ltd.
England

CONTRIBUTORS AND SOURCES:

Don Logan	Lindsay Peacock	Steve Daniels	Picciani Aircraft Slides
Phillip Huston	Bill Malerba	Dave Ostrowski	Flightleader
Gary Meinert	Peter Bergagnini	Mike Campbell	Military Aircraft Photographs
Mike Grove	Arnold Swanberg	Craig Kaston	Centurion Enterprises
Mick Roth	Ben Knowles	Anthony Chong	Eagle Editions, Ltd.
Jim Rotramel	Jerry Geer	Bob LaBouy	GB Aircraft Slides
Tom Brewer	Dwayne Kasulka	Tim White	U. S. Navy
Roy Lock	Hideki Nagakubo	Don Spering/A.I.R.	Department of Defense

Library of Congress Cataloging-in-Publication Data
(Revised for vol. 2)
Kinzey, Bert.
    Colors & markings of U.S. Navy F-4 Phantoms.

    (C&M ; vol. 17, 22)
    Spine title v. 1 : U.S. Navy F-4 Phantoms.
    "A Detail & Scale aviation publication."
    Vol. 2 has imprint: Waukesha, WI : Kalmbach
Books.
    Includes bobliographical references and index.
    Contents: Pt. 1. Atlantic Coast markings -- Pt. 2
Pacific Coast Squadrons.
    1. Phantom II (Jet fighter plane). 2. Airplanes,
Military -- United States -- Identification marks.
3. United States Navy -- Aviation. I. Leader, Ray. II.
Title. III. Title: Colros & Markings of U.S. Navy F-4
Phantoms. IV. Title: U.S. Navy F-4 Phantoms. V.
Series.
UG1242.F5K5484 1991   359.9'4834'0973
90-11314
ISBN 0-8306-4541-1 (pbk : vol. 1)
ISBN 0-85310-624-0 (U.K. : v. 1)
ISBN 0-89024-194-5 (v.2)

First published in Great Britain in 1993
by Airlife Publishing, Ltd.
7 St. John's Hill, Shrewsbury, SY1 1JE

British Library Cataloguing in Publication Data
    A catalogue record for this book
    is available from the British library

ISBN: 1 85310 633 X

Front cover: This beautiful painting was done by well known aviation artist Jerry Crandall. It is entitled "Lightning Strikes Twice," and it depicts an encounter between Phantoms from the USS MIDWAY, CVA-41, and North Vietnamese MiGs on 23 May, 1972. Flying the CAG aircraft from VF-161, LCDR Ron "Mugs" McKeown and his RIO, LT Jack Ensch, shot down two MiG-17s in a battle near Kep Airfield, North Vietnam. Signed and numbered collector's prints of this painting may be ordered by writing to Eagle Editions Ltd., P. O. Box 1830, Sedona, Arizona 86336. In addition to the artist's signature, all prints are autographed by pilot "Mugs" McKeown and RIO Jack Ensch. (Eagle Editions Ltd.)

Rear cover: The contrast between the early colorful paint schemes and the later low-visibility schemes are illustrated in these two photographs. At the top is an F-4N from VF-161 with the gray over white scheme and colorful markings. A red MiG is painted on the splitter plate, and it has a white disc with a red 6 at its center. This is representative of the six MiG kills scored by the squadron in Vietnam. These included four MiG-17s and two MiG-19s. The lower photograph illustrates an F-4N of VF-154 in the colorless markings on the overall gull gray scheme. All markings are a darker gray painted over the lighter gull gray. While the low-visibility paint schemes and subdued markings may improve the survivability of the aircraft in combat, they usually reduce the visual appeal of the aircraft to the viewer and photographer. However, some of the low-visibility and tactical schemes have been made very attractive through the use of small amounts of color and some imagination and artistic planning during the design and application of the gray and black markings. (Both Flightleader)

INTRODUCTION

Very colorful CAG markings are displayed on this F-4N which carries the markings of VF-302. The aircraft is painted in the overall gull gray paint scheme and is shown taxiing out for a training mission in December 1977. Practice bombs are attached to the triple ejector racks on its inboard pylons. The opposite side of this aircraft is illustrated on page 53. *(Lock)*

This publication is intended to be a companion to Colors & Markings of U. S. Navy F-4 Phantoms, Part 1, Atlantic Coast Markings, which is Volume 17 in the Colors & Markings Series. In this new volume is complete coverage of all U. S Navy Phantoms that were based on the Pacific coast. Our presentation is not limited to the squadrons of the Pacific Fleet that flew the Navy versions of the Phantom, but it also includes the three Pacific Naval Reserve Squadrons, two evaluation squadrons, and five Navy test centers located in the western United States.

As with Part 1, we begin with a brief review of the wide variety of paint schemes and markings used on Navy Phantoms throughout their operational service. At one end of the spectrum are some of the most colorful and elaborate schemes ever seen on combat aircraft. These were used during most of the Phantom's service, but over the last several years in which the Navy operated the F-4, there was a steady progression toward less color and low-visibility markings.

Next, we illustrate the Phantoms of the fifteen squadrons in the Pacific Fleet and the three Pacific reserve squadrons. These are arranged in numerical order. It should be noted that three of the fleet squadrons, VF-142, VF-143, and VF-151, are also in Part 1, because they each served a tour aboard Atlantic Fleet carriers using Atlantic Fleet tail codes.

The two evaluation units, VX-4 and VX-5, are covered next. Finally, Phantoms used by the five test and evaluation centers are illustrated. These are the Naval Missile Center, the Pacific Missile Test Center, the Naval Weapons Evaluation Facility, the Parachute Test Center, and the Naval Weapons Center, which are covered in that order.

For each squadron and center, we have made an effort to show a chronology of markings. The reader will therefore be able to study the progressive changes from the colorful and elaborate schemes and markings to the subdued, low-visibility variations that were painted on these aircraft during the final few years of their service life.

A special emphasis has been placed on illustrating CAG aircraft for each fleet and reserve squadron. Other special markings are also shown. Similarly, unique and distinctive paint schemes and camouflage patterns are illustrated. Some one-of-a-kind schemes that were used by VX-4 and VX-5 and by the five test and evaluation centers are also included.

The Phantom is no longer in operational service with the U. S. Navy, so it has become important to provide photographic histories of the various units that flew this classic aircraft and the markings they used. Colors & Markings Volume 17 and this new Volume 22 combine to provide the most extensive coverage of the paint schemes and markings used on U. S. Navy Phantoms that is available anywhere in the world. Nowhere else are the several different schemes and markings used on these aircraft presented on a unit-by-unit basis.

The photographs that are contained in this publication were chosen from several thousand slides, negatives, and prints. Selection was based on providing the most thorough coverage possible for every squadron and center, and very few of the pictures have ever been published before. To assemble this coverage required the efforts, generosity, and cooperation of more than thirty contributors and sources which are listed on page 2. To all of the people who made this book possible, Detail & Scale and the authors extend a sincere word of thanks.

U. S. NAVY F-4 PAINT SCHEMES

The light gull gray over white scheme is nicely illustrated in this in-flight photograph of F-4N, 150444. The gray upper surfaces and the white undersides are clearly visible. VF-161's colorful markings cover the entire vertical stabilizer and rudder. This photograph was taken in January 1976. (Nagakubo)

Shortly after the end of the conflict in Korea, the U. S. Navy decided to replace the overall blue paint scheme that had been used on most of its aircraft since the final stages of World War II. While several different schemes were designed for various types of aircraft, the one selected for fixed-wing, carrier-based aircraft included light gull gray (FS 36440) on the upper surfaces and white on the undersides. All flying surfaces, to include ailerons, flaps, elevators or elevons, and rudders were to be painted white on all sides.

The transition to this scheme took quite some time to accomplish, and for several years in the mid-1950s the Navy's carriers deployed with the aircraft in their air wings painted in a mix of the old and new schemes. During the development of the Phantom, the mock-up was painted overall blue, but by the time the new fighter was ready to fly, the change to the gray over white scheme had been completed.

One of the best features of this new scheme was that it provided a nice neutral background for the addition of elaborate and colorful markings. Although the first generation of infrared-guided missiles had become operational by the time this scheme was adopted, aircraft combat survivability had not become sophisticated enough to consider the use of special paints which would reduce visual and IR signatures. This was really not much of a concern at that time, since the early IR-guided missiles were neither sensitive nor sophisticated enough to home in on anything other than the exhaust from the aircraft's engine. Neither the gray over white scheme nor the colorful markings were effective at reducing an aircraft's visibility to the human eye or to an IR seeker. In the late 1950s, many analysts considered the military might of the United States to be greater than that of all other nations combined. Thus, the addition of colorful and highly visible markings, which ran contrary to any thought of camouflaging the aircraft, reflected the prevailing attitude of the U. S. military at the time. That attitude seemed to be, "Here we are---now what are you going to do about it?"

It was also thought that the new IR and radar-guided air-to-air missiles would mean the end of close-in dogfighting. Analysts believed that in any future combat, engagements would be made beyond visual range (BVR), so what difference would it make if an aircraft was bright and colorful? This same thinking caused the elimination of an internal gun from the original design for the Phantom and other fighters, but the war in Vietnam would eventually prove the errors in this thinking. The requirement to visually identify targets meant that fighters would get close enough to use a gun, so the visual signature of an aircraft remained important. Seeing your enemy before he saw you was a decided advantage, but U. S. Navy aircraft fought throughout the entire war in Vietnam using the gull gray over white scheme with colorful markings. By comparison, the Air Force seemed to have learned this lesson a little faster, and they began painting their silver F-100s, F-104s, F-105s, and other combat aircraft in a new standard camouflage scheme. Although they accepted their first Phantoms in the

Navy's gray over white scheme, the Air Force soon painted these aircraft in their standard camouflage as well. The Navy did in fact experiment with a few camouflage schemes during the Vietnam War, but this was done on a very limited basis, and none of the tests resulted in any official adoption of camouflage for the Navy's aircraft.

When aircraft were received by the various Navy squadrons in the gray over white scheme, personnel seemed anxious to use as much colorful paint as possible for the unit's special markings. Often, these markings were designed to accentuate the lines of the particular type of aircraft that the unit operated. In the case of the Phantom, the big fighter's unique features offered ample opportunity and space for the artists in each unit to use their imaginations in designing and applying markings. Sometimes, the new markings were based on those previously used by the unit on Crusaders, Demons, and other earlier fighters, but many squadrons designed completely new sets of markings for the Phantom. It is also interesting to note that some squadrons made substantial changes to the markings used on their Phantoms over the years. However, other units that flew the various Navy versions of the F-4 for as long as two decades made few if any changes in their squadron markings.

As the Phantom entered service, the early squadron markings were usually rather conservative. But as time passed, it sometimes seemed as if one squadron was trying to outdo the others. This was particularly true of sister squadrons that served together aboard the same carrier. Often the entire vertical tail and rudder were covered completely with squadron colors. Markings sometimes ran the entire length of the spine of the aircraft, while others were added to wing tips and to the sides of the fuselage. There can be little doubt that maintenance personnel spent a lot of time with their aircraft, first applying these elaborate markings, then maintaining them in good condition. Regardless of the time required, Navy aircraft were usually maintained in an excellent appearance except when they were exposed to the elements during lengthy deployments at sea and in combat.

Fortunately, the colorful markings were still in vogue and approved for Navy aircraft in 1976 when America celebrated its two-hundredth birthday. Almost every unit painted at least one of its aircraft with special markings in honor of this historic event. Although some of these markings consisted of only the bi-centennial star, which was known as the "pretzel," many aircraft were painted in very elaborate markings. These added to the visual appeal of the aircraft, and Phantoms had some of the most attractive bi-centennial schemes and markings ap-

Non-standard paint schemes were also applied to Navy Phantoms, and among the most colorful of these were those applied during 1976 to help celebrate America's two-hundredth birthday. F-4J, 153088, was painted by VX-4 in this elaborate and beautiful scheme that covered the entire aircraft. The special markings on this aircraft are further illustrated on page 58. (Rotramel)

As air combat survivability dictated the need to reduce the visual and infrared signatures of aircraft, the gull gray over white scheme was replaced with the overall gull gray scheme. Markings were usually, but not always, limited to grays and blacks. Here, F-4S, 153858, shows markings of a similar design to those used when extensive amounts of color were prevalent, but now a dark gray is used instead for all unit markings. But note that the national insignia and the NAVY are still quite large, and the unit markings cover the entire vertical tail and rudder. This was the first step in the evolution to the truly low-visibility markings of the tactical schemes.   *(Flightleader Collection)*

plied to any type of aircraft.

But in the late 1970s, the need to consider air combat survivability was emphasized, and a rather lengthy but steady transition to paint schemes and markings with reduced visual and IR signatures was begun. Even the types of paints and their formulas were studied to reduce reflectivity.

Unlike the Air Force, the Navy did not select a camouflage of several colors which were painted in an irregular pattern for its aircraft. Instead, the highly reflective white undersides of the aircraft were painted with the same light gull gray paint that had been used on the upper surfaces. The control surfaces were also painted light gull gray, leaving only the insides of the wheel wells, the landing gear, and the interior of the air intakes the same white as they had been previously. At first, the gray was usually quite glossy, and colorful markings remained the norm. However, the amount of color used by most squadrons was reduced by varying degrees.

It was not long before the gloss began to disappear from the overall gray scheme, and the color used for the markings was decreased considerably. Even the national insignia was often painted gray along with the rest of the markings. Only rarely was any appreciable amount of color painted on an aircraft, and even then it seemed to lack the luster or gloss used previously.

At first, the new gray markings were as large as

they had been when color was used, but low-visibility also soon meant a reduction in size as well. The national insignia and the word NAVY on the sides of the fuselage were reduced to only a fraction of their previous size. In fact, they became very difficult, if not impossible, to see at any distance. No longer could the national insignia be considered as an aid in the recognition of the aircraft with respect to friend or foe. Unit markings likewise became smaller on many aircraft, and except in very rare instances, only grays and black were used for these markings.

The progression from the colorful schemes to those designed to reduce visibility was not a step-by-step process. For several years in the late 1970s and early 1980s, an observer could walk out on any ramp and see aircraft from the same squadron in several different schemes on any given day. Some Phantoms could be seen with varying amounts of color, while others would have only gray and black markings. Like the change from the overall blue to the gull gray over white scheme, the transition to low-visibility was gradual and without clearly defined stages.

During the time the Navy was officially moving toward low-visibility schemes and markings, it again experimented with a few camouflage patterns. Most noteworthy of these were the angular geometric patterns of various shades of gray designed by aviation artist Keith Ferris. These were applied to

Four different shades of gray were painted on this F-4S from VF-302. VF-301 also had aircraft painted in similar schemes as illustrated on page 51. These graded camouflage patterns were developed by CDR C. J. "Heater" Heatley, who was possibly inspired by the geometric Ferris schemes. Although unofficial, pilots reported that these graded schemes were among the most effective ever applied to the Phantom. Additional photographs of VF-302's Phantoms in these graded schemes can be found on page 54.

(Kaston)

Air Force as well as Navy aircraft, but none were ever adopted for official widespread use. Similar schemes of graded grays were developed by CDR C. J. "Heater" Heatley who was well known for his aviation photography. Several variations of this type of camouflage were used by Naval Reserve squadrons VF-301 and VF-302 for a short time in the early 1980s.

By the time the Navy was adopting official tactical paint schemes for its aircraft, the Phantom was nearing the twilight of its career. Most squadrons that had flown the F-4 had already transitioned to the F-14 Tomcat or were in the process of doing so. Some of these units were disestablished as the Navy reduced the number of aircraft carriers in service. Among the last Phantom squadrons in the regular Navy were those assigned to the USS MIDWAY, CV-41, and the USS CORAL SEA, CV-43. These smaller carriers were not capable of effectively operating the larger F-14, so Phantoms remained in the air wings of these two ships until the F/A-18 Hornet was available as a replacement. The squadrons assigned to the MIDWAY and CORAL SEA wore the low-visibility schemes longer than any other fleet units. It should be noted that both of these carriers have now been withdrawn from service. While an official tactical scheme was actually designed for the Phantom by the Air Combat Surviv-

ability Branch, it was never applied to many aircraft. Instead, the low-visibility overall gray scheme appears to have been the last official paint scheme to be applied to the aircraft on anything but a rather limited basis.

Phantoms used by the Navy's test and evaluation centers and facilities often carried the same paint schemes as those applied to the aircraft in the fleet and reserve squadrons. However, these organizations also took some liberties when it came to painting and marking many of the various types of aircraft they flew. Some of their schemes became very well known and were the subjects of very extensive photography and model building. Among these were the overall black Phantoms of VX-4 with the white Playboy bunny markings as illustrated on page 57. The unit's overall white aircraft with the gray bunny was likewise well known. High-visibility markings were painted on QF-4 drones, and in a number of cases, the entire aircraft was painted in a bright red-orange.

From the colorful to the subdued, from the elaborate to the plain, and from the common to the unique, the widely varied paint schemes of the U. S. Navy's Pacific coast Phantoms are interesting to the aviation historian, enthusiast, and model builder alike. Coverage of these schemes and markings begins on the following page with VF-21.

VF-21 FREELANCERS

The Freelancers of VF-21 transitioned to F-4B Phantoms in late 1962. This photograph of F-4B, 151478, was taken in November 1967, and although it has no special markings, it was being used as the squadron's CAG aircraft at that time.
(Picciani Aircraft Slides)

Standard squadron markings for VF-21 are displayed on F-4B, 151472. However, the unit's insignia has not been added to the chevron on the tail. The two-tone radomes seen on this aircraft and the one shown above are interesting. The forward section of the radome is cream colored, while the aft section and the addition to the IR sensor beneath the radome are white. (Flightleader)

VF-21 had transitioned to F-4Js by the time this photograph was taken of 155741. However, the squadron still operated as part of Carrier Air Wing Two which was assigned to the USS RANGER, CV-61. This was the CAG aircraft as indicated by the **100** modex and the words **COMMANDER AIR WING TWO** stencilled on the side of the fuselage. Note that the markings had not been changed from those shown above on the F-4Bs. However, the radomes on the squadron's F-4Js were black.
(Flightleader)

This in-flight photograph of F-4J, 158356, illustrates the changes that had taken place in VF-21's markings by the early 1970s. A yellow chevron with a black outline had replaced the previous black chevron, and a black panther on a lance had replaced the squadron insignia within the chevron. Although the markings had been changed, the squadron remained assigned to the USS RANGER. *(U. S. Navy)*

Another one of VF-21's Phantoms is seen at right. Notice the change in the black anti-glare panel that now curves back from the radome at the bottom. Compare this to the standard anti-glare panel and radome seen on the aircraft above. *(Flightleader)*

VF-21 had adopted more colorful markings for its CAG aircraft by the time 158378 was photographed at Edwards AFB, California, on 13 November, 1977. Colorful stars had been added to the aircraft's rudder. *(Logan)*

By November 1978, the Freelancer's Phantoms were painted in the new overall gray scheme as seen in this photograph. The markings remained the same as they had been on the gray over white scheme.

(Flightleader)

New markings for the CAG aircraft are illustrated in this photograph which was taken in February 1979. CAG had been painted in black letters at the top of the rudder above the colorful stars. Notice that this aircraft has a gray replacement radome instead of one in the usual black. *(Huston)*

VF-21's markings had undergone yet another change by late 1980. The squadron had changed to **NK** tail codes which were painted in black with a yellow shadow. This change in tail codes was necessitated by the squadron's reassignment to the air wing aboard the USS CORAL SEA, although the carrier's name had not been added to this aircraft. *(Meinert)*

VF-21 had transitioned to F-4Ns when this CAG aircraft was photographed in May 1981. **USS CORAL SEA** was painted on the fuselage in black. *(Grove)*

Another VF-21 CAG Phantom was photographed as it returned from a training mission. Notice that the squadron had changed to low-visibility gray markings by the time this photograph was taken in October 1982. All markings were in black or a very dark gray.

(Grove)

VF-22L1

VF-22L1 was a Navy Reserve squadron that was assigned to NAS Los Alamitos, California. The squadron operated F-4Bs from 1969 until late 1970, being the first Naval Reserve squadron to fly the Phantom. F-4B, 148385, illustrates the red and white checkerboard pattern that was on the rudder and horizontal stabilizers of the unit's Phantoms.   *(Picciani Aircraft Slides)*

Not all of VF-22L1's Phantoms received the checkerboard markings, as evidenced by 158369 in the background of this photograph. A *7L* tail code was painted in black on each aircraft.

(Flightleader Collection)

VF-51 SCREAMING EAGLES

The Screaming Eagles of VF-51 transitioned from the F-8J Crusader to the F-4B Phantom in 1971. Their early CAG markings are illustrated on F-4B, 153009. The stylized eagle painted across the fuselage was maroon with multi-colored tail feathers. Because of the eagle's long slender shape and the design of its beak, it was often referred to as the "supersonic can opener." *COMMANDER ATTACK CARRIER AIR WING FIFTEEN* was painted in black below the eagle.   (Flightleader Collection)

A well worn Phantom displays the standard markings for VF-51. Except for the CAG aircraft, the eagle's tail feathers were alternating maroon and white. *MAD DOG* was painted in white on the maroon fin cap.   (Flightleader)

F-4B, 150417, was photographed in August 1971. The same maroon color was used to paint the eagle, fin cap, and travel pod. The black *NL* tail code was also shadowed in the same color. Note the carrier's name *USS CORAL SEA* lettered in black on the eagle.   (Picciani Aircraft Slides)

VF-51 had made a major change to their squadron markings by the time this photograph was taken at NAS Miramar, California, in December 1972. The black tail had red **NL** tail codes and the black rudder was edged in red. Notice the CAG stripes applied to the rudder. **COMMANDER CVW 15, VF 51,** and **USS CORAL SEA** are stencilled on the fuselage in black.   (Roth via Picciani)

The Screaming Eagles were still assigned to the USS CORAL SEA when this photograph was taken in 1972. One of their Phantoms was photographed at NAS Miramar, California, and it illustrates the unit's standard markings at that time.   (Brewer)

Because the red outline of the **NL** tail code was difficult to see, it was subsequently changed to white as shown here on F-4B, 151459. This photograph was taken in 1974.

(Military Aircraft Photographs)

The Screaming Eagles had transitioned to the F-4N by the time this Phantom was photographed on 18 November, 1975. Notice the change in the CAG markings that are painted on the tail. (Brewer)

An unusual style of CAG markings had been applied to F-4B, 151503. The **NL** tail codes were painted in white, and white **00**s were located at the front of the tail. On the nose, **GAA** was lettered in black, while a black **100** modex appeared on the splitter plate.

(Centurion Enterprises)

VF-51's bi-centennial markings were very colorful and patriotic. F-4N, 150476, had red, white, and blue tail bands and a blue disc on the nose with white stars and a white **76**. (Roth)

This close-up of 150476 provides a look at some of the special markings that are obscured by the folded wing panel in the photograph above. These include the red, white, and blue **76** and the words **SCREAMING EAGLES** in red, white, and blue script on the side of the fuselage. **VF-51** and **USS CORAL SEA** were painted in red and shadowed in black. (Roth)

This photograph of 150476 illustrates the change to **NM** tail codes. A small squadron zap was applied to the upper corner of the splitter plate. The carrier's name was removed from the side of the fuselage because the squadron had been reassigned. Evidently the unit's designation was also painted out at the same time. (Lock)

F-4N, 152267, displayed CAG markings when this photograph was taken on 10 March, 1975. These included a colorful set of horizontal stripes which were painted across the tail and rudder. (Peacock)

In December 1977, a different Phantom was being used as the squadron's CAG's aircraft. Notice the change to the **NM** tail code and the MiG kill marking which is painted on the splitter plate in the form of a red star. (Malerba Collection)

F-4N, 153067, illustrates the standard markings for VF-51 after the change to the **NM** tail code. This is the squadron commander's aircraft, and it was photographed on 29 October, 1977. (Bergagnini)

VF-92 SILVER KINGS

Early markings for the Silver Kings of VF-92 are illustrated on F-4B, 151443. The king chess piece on the tail was painted in silver to denote the unit's name.
(Flightleader Collection)

By August 1972, VF-92 had transitioned to F-4Js. Their CAG aircraft displays the yellow squadron colors on the tail and wing tips. Notice the multi-colored cards and aces behind the canopy that serve as CAG markings.
(Lock)

This right front view of F-4J, 155569, depicts typical squadron markings for the Silver Kings. The VF-92 and the 206 modex were painted black and shadowed with yellow.
(Lock)

VF-92 subsequently made more changes to their markings as evidenced by this photograph of F-4J, 153882, which was taken in April 1974. This Phantom was the squadron's CAG aircraft and had special markings on the tail. Notice that the entire vertical tail was painted yellow with the squadron insignia located within a black spade.

(Swanberg)

Another change had occurred by the time F-4J, 153842, was photographed on 25 April, 1974. The **NG** tail code was a different style than the one on the aircraft at the top of this page. Instead of having a black chevron, the leading edge of the tail was painted black. The anti-glare panel extended from the nose onto the canopy rails and back past the rear cockpit.

(Brewer)

VF-96 FIGHTING FALCONS

The Fighting Falcons of VF-96 were deployed aboard the USS ENTERPRISE, CVA(N)-65, when this photograph was taken. At that time the squadron was still operating the F-4B. Notice the squadron's MiG kills painted in white on the black triangle at the front of the vertical tail. (Spering/A.I.R. Collection)

After transitioning from the F-4B to the F-4J, VF-96 made no changes to their markings. This photograph illustrates the right side of one of their F-4Js in CAG markings. These included a row of multi-colored stars on the side of the fuselage. (Flightleader)

The opposite side of the same aircraft is illustrated here. However, note that the carrier assignment had been changed to the USS AMERICA, CVA-66. (Flightleader Collection)

VF-96 had been reassigned to the USS CONSTELLATION, CVA-64, by the time this photograph was taken. There are eight MiG kill markings painted on the splitter plate in the form of small North Vietnamese flags. These kill markings represent the squadron's kills rather that any scored in this particular aircraft. The aircraft is shown here as it appeared in 1972.

(Military Aircraft Photographs)

F-4J, 155541, was not a MiG killer, but like the Phantom shown above, it also displays the squadron's kills on the splitter plate. This was a common practice for several squadrons during and shortly after the war in Vietnam.

(Knowles)

This view of 155580 shows the Fighting Falcons CAG markings very clearly. The white centerline tank had a stylized Falcon painted on it. Also note that the MiG kill markings had been deleted by the time this photograph was taken in April 1975. These are the last markings used by the VF-96, which was disestablished in November 1975.

(Brewer)

VF-111 SUNDOWNERS

The Sundowners of VF-111 painted markings on their Phantoms that were among the most colorful and popular of any used by the squadrons of the Pacific Fleet. This CAG aircraft had multi-colored stars at the top of the vertical stabilizer. *(Logan)*

The right side of F-4B, 151464, illustrates the early squadron markings for the Sundowners. At first, the setting sun and its rays were only painted on the rudder. *(Flightleader)*

Later, VF-111 painted the sunburst across the entire vertical tail and rudder. A black MiG silhouette was painted on the splitter plate to indicate a victory over a North Vietnamese MiG. It was scored in this aircraft on 6 March, 1972, by LT Garry Weigand and his RIO, LTJG Bill Freckleton. The kill was scored against a MiG-17.
(Geer Collection)

VF-111 painted F-4N, 151000, in CAG markings which consisted of multi-colored rays passing through the **NL** tail code. This photograph was taken at NAS Miramar, California, in October 1975. (Kasulka)

Some minor changes were made to the Sundowner's markings for America's bi-centennial celebration. One of the sun's rays was changed to red, white, and blue. Thirteen white stars and a white **76** were added to the sun. (Roth)

The right side of F-4N, 150475, further illustrates the bi-centennial markings painted on the aircraft. However, notice that the tail code had been changed to **NM** and the carrier name **USS ROOSEVELT** was painted in black on the fuselage. The carrier was the USS FRANKLIN D. ROOSEVELT, CVA-42, and it should not be confused with the present USS THEODORE ROOSEVELT, CVN-71. This photograph is dated June 1976.

(Grove)

A well worn and tired CAG aircraft also reflected the changes in markings after the squadron was reassigned to USS ROOSEVELT. This aircraft was photographed in May 1977 after that carrier made its last deployment and had been retired from service. The Sundowners transitioned to the F-14 Tomcat the following year.

(Flightleader)

VF-114 AARDVARKS

VF-114 was one of the first squadrons to operate the Phantom, and they received some of the early F4H-1 variant. One of these aircraft, F4H-1, 148391, is shown here as it appeared in early 1962. The original F4H-1 designation is above the bureau number, and the word **NAVY** is lettered above it in small letters. The only squadron color was on the fin cap which was painted orange. (Flightleader Collection)

This photograph of F-4B, 148409, was taken in August 1964, and it illustrates an early CAG aircraft flown by VF-114. **USS KITTY HAWK COMMANDER CARRIER AIR WING ELEVEN** was lettered on the sides of the fuselage in black. A small white Aardvark was painted on the multi-colored fin cap.

(Picciani Aircraft Slides)

The well known and popular markings used by the Aardvarks for many years had made their appearance by the time this photograph was taken. These included a large orange Aardvark on the vertical tail. An orange band with black borders was painted diagonally across the fuselage. The orange shield on the splitter plate had the name **PATTY** lettered in black.

(Flightleader Collection)

VF-114 had transitioned to the F-4J by the time this photograph was taken on 10 June, 1973. The Aardvarks simply continued to use the same markings that had been painted on their F-4Bs. *(Kasulka)*

The Aardvark's CAG aircraft sported stars of various colors on the white rudder. **COMMANDER ATTACK CARRIER AIR WING ELEVEN USS KITTY HAWK CVA-63** was lettered on the fuselage in black.
(Flightleader Collection)

This photograph of F-4J, 157246, shows the typical squadron markings and their locations on the left side of the aircraft.
(Flightleader Collection)

VF-121 PACEMAKERS

VF-121 was the RAG (Replacement Air Group) for Pacific Fleet F-4 squadrons, and as such was the first Pacific squadron to transition to the Phantom. It received its first F4H-1 in late 1960, and one of its first aircraft is illustrated here after the designation had been changed to F-4A. The only unit markings were the black **NJ** tail code and the **VF-121** above the **NAVY** on the fuselage.

(Military Aircraft Photographs)

This photograph of F-4B, 152988, shows the addition of flaming black panthers on the fuselage and wing tanks.

(Flightleader Collection)

One of VF-121's early F-4Bs was still being used for on-the-job-training when it was photographed in January 1976. Although they are a little faded, the markings used by the Pacemakers during the early 1970s are visible. Notice the emblem on the tail which contained **FRAMP** in black.   (Grove)

This Phantom was marked as the air wing commander's aircraft for VF-121, and it had **COMFIT AEWWINGPAC** lettered in black above the red flash on the fuselage. (Flightleader Collection)

A different wing commander's aircraft is shown here as it appeared in the early 1970s. It had a multi-colored rudder and the words **COMMANDER READINESS ATTACK CARRIER AIR WING TWELVE** lettered on the upper fuselage. (Flightleader Collection)

A third wing commander's aircraft is seen in this photograph of F-4J, 155794. Notice the multi-colored stars on the white rudder. **RADM L.A. SNEAD** was stencilled in black on the canopy rail, and two white stars on a dark blue field were located on the splitter plate. **COMFITAEWWINGPAC** was lettered in black above the red flash on the fuselage.
(Flightleader Collection)

*By June 1976, a different aircraft was used for the wing commander, however, the same name, **RADM L.A. SNEAD,** was lettered in black on the canopy rail. The squadron's insignia was applied to the tail, and red, white, and blue diagonal stripes were on the rudder along with a small red chevron. **SWOOSE** was painted in white on the red fin cap.* (Logan)

F-4J, 153803, was photographed while operating on the flight deck of the USS RANGER on 14 December, 1976. (Lock)

At left is a close-up of the right side of the tail showing the markings that VF-121 used on its aircraft during 1976. At right is a look at the markings on the left side. The pilot's call sign was stencilled in white on the left side of the red fin cap, while the RIO's name was on the right side. (Left Grove, right Kinzey)

At first glance, this may appear to be the same photograph seen on the previous page, but it is of a different aircraft with different markings. Red, white, and blue horizontal stripes were painted on the rudder, replacing the diagonal stripes seen earlier. The fin cap was no longer red, but had horizontal red, white, and blue stripes. The flash had been removed from the fuselage, but one had been added to the forward corner of the vertical tail. *(Lock)*

A black panther had been added to the fuselage of the Pacemakers aircraft by December 1977. *(Lock)*

VF-121 changed over to low visibility gray markings and the overall gray paint scheme by July 1980. *(Flightleader)*

VF-142 GHOSTRIDERS

The early markings used by the Ghostriders of VF-142 are illustrated on F-4B, 151413. The squadron was assigned to the air wing aboard the USS CONSTELLATION, and it used the **NK** tail code.

(Picciani Aircraft Slides)

This view of the left side of F-4B, 150417, further illustrates the markings applied to the Ghostrider's Phantoms.

(Lock)

The Ghostriders retained the same markings after transitioning to the F-4J as shown here. In fact, except for changing the carrier names, the squadron used virtually the same markings for all of its deployments aboard carriers of the Pacific Fleet. However, for its cruise aboard USS AMERICA, CV-66, with the Atlantic Fleet, its markings were quite different. (See page 39 in Colors & Markings of U. S. Navy F-4 Phantoms, Part 1, Atlantic Coast Markings.)

(Flightleader)

VF-142 made several cruises to Vietnam. Three of these combat deployments were aboard the USS CON-STELLATION. Here, one of the unit's F-4Js is being checked over prior to a mission. Note the Sidewinder missiles on the inboard pylon.

(Flightleader Collection)

Using the same markings, the Ghostriders also embarked in USS ENTERPRISE for a combat tour. The only difference in markings was the change in the carrier's name which was located on the upper fuselage.

(Flightleader Collection)

VF-143 PUKIN' DOGS

The earliest markings for the Pukin' Dogs of VF-143 are illustrated in this photograph that was taken in May 1963. At this time the large winged pukin' dog was painted on the side of the fuselage just behind the national insignia. Four small white pukin' dogs were also painted on the blue fin cap.

(Picciani Aircraft Slides)

Later, the unit changed to the markings illustrated on F-4B, 152282. The carrier name **USS CONSTELLA-TION** was painted in black on the fuselage. The pukin' dog was moved to the tail, and the tail code was offset diagonally instead of being horizontal as shown above. The small white pukin' dogs had been removed from the fin cap.

(Flightleader Collection)

A transition to the F-4J variant of the Phantom had taken place by 1969, however, the same markings were retained. Below the carrier's name was a large black E and **BEST IN THE WEST**.
(Military Aircraft Photographs)

VF-143 made one of its seven combat deployments to Vietnam aboard the USS ENTERPRISE. These are the markings used during that cruise. Note the carrier's name on the upper fuselage with the long blue flash that extends from just behind the cockpits to the tail section. The pukin' dog was moved back to the fuselage.
(Flightleader Collection)

This photograph shows the markings on the left side of the aircraft. Like the photograph immediately above, these are the makings used by the unit while deployed aboard the USS ENTERPRISE. The squadron also deployed to Vietnam aboard the USS AMERICA, one of the carriers of the Atlantic Fleet. The markings used during that cruise are illustrated on page 40 of Colors & Markings of U. S. Navy F-4 Phantoms, Part 1, Atlantic Coast Markings. However, those markings were the same as the ones shown here, except that the carrier's name read **USS AMERICA** and the tail code was **AJ** instead of the **NK** seen in this photograph.
(Flightleader Collection)

VF-151 FIGHTING VIGILANTES

The Vigilantes of VF-151 transitioned to the F-4B in 1964 and were assigned to the USS CORAL SEA, CVA-43, for seven tours to the Gulf of Tonkin during the Vietnam War. This F-4B, 153913, depicts the early markings used by this unit. VF-151 also flew F-4Bs with the Atlantic Fleet for a short period of time. See page 41 in Colors & Markings of U. S. Navy F-4 Phantoms, Part 1, Atlantic Coast Markings, for photographs of the two different paint schemes that the squadron used during that time. *(Flightleader Collection)*

A significant change in the squadron's markings is illustrated in this photograph of VF-151's CAG aircraft. The entire vertical tail and rudder had multi-colored stripes for CAG markings. The **NL** tail code was black with a white outline. **COMMANDER ATTACK CARRIER AIR WING FIFTEEN** was lettered on the upper fuselage in black.

(Flightleader Collection)

The squadron was later reassigned to the USS MIDWAY, CVA-41. Notice that the tail code has been changed to **NF** to signify the squadron's reassignment to CVW-5. On the fuselage **COMMANDER ATTACK CARRIER AIR WING FIVE** and **USS MIDWAY** are lettered in black. This is a different CAG aircraft from that seen in the photo at left, although the multi-colored tail markings remain the same.

(Flightleader Collection)

One of VF-151's Phantoms was photographed as it made its landing approach. The standard squadron colors were painted on the tail of this aircraft. *(Flightleader Collection)*

The squadron had transitioned to F-4Ns when 151400 was photographed in the landing pattern on 19 May, 1977. This is the CAG aircraft, and the various colors on the tail are more difficult to discern than those shown on the previous page because they are not separated with thin white lines. (Nagakubo)

The squadron was well represented during the bi-centennial celebration by F-4N, 150452, which was also the squadron commander's aircraft. Red, white, and blue were not only found in the beautiful tail markings. These patriotic colors were also used for the modex, the carrier's name, and the stripes on the canopy rails. (Nagakubo)

This Phantom had the Vigilantes standard markings as of May 1977. The tail is painted yellow and black. (Nagakubo)

VF-151 transitioned to F-4Js in late 1977, but the same markings used on the F-4Ns were retained. This view of F-4J, 155579, was taken aboard the USS MIDWAY. (Daniels)

The squadron then transitioned to the F-4S in 1980. This slatted-wing Phantom was photographed in the landing pattern at NAF Atsugi, Japan, on 3 June, 1981. The markings painted on the tail had been changed, and the aircraft was painted in the overall gray scheme. (Nagakubo)

VF-154 BLACK KNIGHTS

Although VF-154 operated all four Navy fighter versions of the Phantom over a period of twenty years between 1966 and 1986, its markings changed very little until the introduction of the low-visibility schemes. F-4J, 158373, was painted in markings for the CAG of CVW-2 when photographed in February 1975. The unit's standard markings were supplemented with multi-colored stripes on the rudder for the CAG. **COMMANDER ATTACK CARRIER AIR WING TWO** was lettered on the side of the fuselage. The Black Knights were assigned to the USS RANGER at that time. *(Lock)*

Another of VF-154's Phantoms was photographed while flying at NAS Miramar, California, on 2 May, 1975. The unit's standard markings are illustrated here. *(Bergagnini)*

This photograph of the right side of F-4J 155761 shows the squadron's markings on the opposite side of the aircraft. *(Flightleader)*

The Black Knights had transitioned to the F-4S when this photograph was taken at Nellis AFB, Nevada, on 14 June, 1980. One of the small changes that did occur to the unit's markings over the years can be seen here. To reflect the change in air wing assignment, the tail code had been changed to **NK**. This tail code is smaller than the **NE** used previously, and is further forward on the orange and black tail flash. The aircraft is painted in the overall gray scheme but retains colorful markings and insignias. (Flightleader)

Because the slatted F-4S proved less than satisfactory on the smaller decks of the MIDWAY class carriers, VF-154 transitioned to the F-4N and continued to operate aboard the USS CORAL SEA. F-4N, 153065, was the squadron's CAG aircraft in May 1981, however it has only the unit's standard markings on the overall gray scheme. (GB Aircraft Slides)

The squadrons assigned to the CORAL SEA were changing to the tactical paint scheme and low-visibility markings when 151431 was photographed as it taxied in from a flight. Even with this change, the unit retained the same design for its markings that it had used over the years. (Grove)

VF-161 CHARGERS

The Chargers of VF-161 transitioned from the F-3B (formerly F3H-2) Demon to the F-4B Phantom in late 1964. F-4B, 151006, is shown here in the early markings used by this squadron in 1968. At this time the unit was assigned to the air wing aboard the USS CORAL SEA.   (Picciani Aircraft Slides)

The squadron also operated aboard the USS MIDWAY during the latter part of the war in Vietnam, and it eventually accumulated six MiG kills. F-4B, 153045, displays the squadron's MiG kills on the splitter plate. The black MiG silhouette had a white **5** painted on it with **THE MIG KILLERS** in black located below the kill marking. The squadron had also changed markings and acquired the **NF** tail code after reassignment to the MIDWAY. It would retain these markings with very little change throughout the rest of the time it operated Phantoms.

(Spering/A.I.R. Collection)

The squadron had changed to the F-4N when this Phantom was photographed while landing in May 1977. F-4N, 151433, was the CAG aircraft and had multi-colored lightning bolts on its rudder. The black characters on the splitter plate are Japanese for CAG. Also note that the carrier's name is multi-colored.
(Nagakubo)

*The Chargers' standard markings are illustrated on this F-4N. **USS MIDWAY** was painted in white on the black fuselage band.*
(Flightleader Collection)

VF-161 wasn't to be outdone by its sister squadron, VF-151, during America's bi-centennial celebration. F-4N, 151433, displays its patriotic colors in this photograph which was taken in April 1976.   (Daniels)

After transitioning to the F-4J, the Chargers changed to the overall gray scheme but retained the same standard markings that they had used for years. F-4J, 158372, was photographed on final approach at NAF Atsugi, Japan, in May 1979. *(Nagakubo)*

VF-161 transitioned to the F-4S in 1980, and the change to the low-visibility paint scheme and markings is evident in this photograph of F-4S, 153808. All markings, to include the lightning bolt on the tail, are in various shades of gray. *(U. S. Navy)*

F-4S, 153808, was photographed in June 1980. Since this is the CAG aircraft for the unit, the lightning bolt remains in red with a white outline. There are no other special CAG markings. *(Flightleader)*

VF-191 SATAN'S KITTENS

After flying Crusaders during eight combat cruises to Vietnam, VF-191 transitioned to the Phantom in early 1976. However, they were disestablished only two years later. During their short time in F-4Js, they marked their squadron commander's aircraft with these attractive bi-centennial markings. (Lock)

This Phantom was painted in the standard squadron markings used by VF-191. The red stripe on the tail contained three white diamonds. A large red diamond was painted on the white rudder.
(Roth)

The squadron's CAG aircraft was photographed while landing at NAF Atsugi in April 1977. The red tail stripe had multi-colored diamonds for the CAG.
(Nagakubo)

VF-194 RED LIGHTNINGS

VF-191's sister squadron was VF-194, and they too had flown Crusaders during the war in Vietnam. Like VF-191, the Red Lightnings operated F-4Js for about two years. This photo illustrates their unadorned CAG aircraft in standard squadron markings.
(Logan)

This right side view of F-4J, 153878, further illustrates the squadron's simple but attractive markings. This is the squadron commander's aircraft.
(Flightleader)

In 1977, VF-194 experimented with some gray camouflage paint schemes. F-J, 153798, was photographed with one of these schemes on 12 February, 1977. Note the squadron markings on the tail which are simply outlines of the lightning bolt and tail code. *(Lock)*

This high view of 153798 provides a good look at the camouflage pattern on the top of the aircraft. *(Roth)*

The right side of the same aircraft is shown in this photograph taken on 28 October, 1976. *(Roth)*

VF-213 BLACK LIONS

The Black Lions of VF-213 transitioned to the F-4B in 1964 after flying Demons for several years. This photograph of F-4B, 152260, was taken in September 1965 and displays the typical squadron markings used at that time. *(Picciani Aircraft Slides)*

Photographed while operating over Vietnam, this Phantom shows the markings painted on the left side of VF-213's aircraft. *(U. S. Navy)*

This photograph illustrates a change in VF-213's markings. The chevron and fin cap were red, and the **NH** tail code and squadron emblem were black. The carrier name **USS KITTY HAWK** was lettered in black on the fuselage.
(Flightleader Collection)

The Black Lions transitioned to the F-4J in 1970, but the unit continued to use markings that were very similar to the last markings that had been used on its F-4Bs. This Phantom was photographed just before VF-213 transitioned to the F-14 Tomcat. The squadron emblem was painted on a dark blue background.
(Roth)

The fin cap on the Black Lion's CAG aircraft had multi-colored bands. **COMMANDER ATTACK CARRIER AIR WING ELEVEN USS KITTY HAWK** was stencilled in black near the top of the fuselage. (Flightleader Collection)

Photographed on 1 October, 1974, aboard the USS AMERICA, F-4J, 155880, still retained the **NH** tail code and **USS KITTY HAWK** markings in black. This was a temporary Atlantic Fleet deployment for the purpose of participating in Exercise Northern Merger.
(Peacock)

47

VF-301 DEVIL'S DISCIPLES

Navy Reserve squadron VF-301 transitioned from Crusaders to the F-4B in mid-1974. This Phantom was photographed in August of that year, shortly after the transition was completed. The red arrow on the tail was edged with black. Like most of the Pacific Fleet F-4 squadrons, Navy Reserve squadron VF-301 was shore based at NAS Miramar, California. *(Ostrowski)*

This left side view of F-4B, 153010, illustrates the squadron markings on the opposite side of the aircraft. As with other Pacific reserve squadrons, VF-301 used the stylized **ND** tail code with the **D** actually being in the form of the Greek letter Delta. *(Bergagnini)*

VF-301's CAG aircraft had special bi-centennial markings when photographed in March 1976. The multi-colored stars at the base of the vertical tail are for the CAG, while the bi-centennial markings are on the side of the fuselage. *(Lock)*

The Devil's Disciples usual CAG markings were painted on F-4N, 152278. Instead of having the bicentennial markings that are illustrated on the previous page, a large red arrow with multi-colored stars was painted on the fuselage. The stars were also at the base of the vertical tail. (Bergagnini)

The right side of the same CAG aircraft is shown here. (Logan)

This left rear view of 151456 gives a better look at the stylized **ND** tail code and the unit's standard markings. (Bergagnini)

This Phantom was photographed in late 1977, and it illustrates the change to the overall gray scheme. However, the squadron's colorful markings remain the same as they had been on the gray over white scheme. Note that the **VF-301** on the fuselage is black with a white shadow. (Flightleader)

This overall gray Phantom has the same markings as the one shown above, however the squadron's designation on the fuselage is not shadowed with white. (Grove)

VF-301 had transitioned to the F-4S by the time 153884 was photographed in early 1982.. The squadron had started using the low visibility paint scheme, and its markings are in a shade of gray only slightly darker than the background color. This makes them very difficult to see even in this color photograph. (Grove)

F-4S, 155878, was photographed in May 1983 when the was unit using the graded camouflage scheme developed by CDR C. J. "Heater" Heatley. These grays included FS 36307, 36375, 35237, and 35164 from the lightest to the darkest. The stylized arrow on the tail had been reduced to a red outline.

(Grove)

A different Phantom is shown here in the graded camouflage scheme, and it was photographed on the transit ramp at NAS Oceana, Virginia, on 5 May, 1984. Most markings on this aircraft were painted in black, except for the outline of the red arrow. The aircraft shows some signs of weathering and spot painting by different colors or with paint which had not yet weathered.

(Campbell)

At left is a view of F-4S, 155749, which had a black MiG kill marking on the rear fuselage. At right is a close-up of the same aircraft taken a year later that shows the addition of the North Vietnamese flag to the black MiG kill. *THE KILLER* is also in black and appears to be hand written. This aircraft is credited with a MiG-17 on 10 May, 1972, while assigned to VF-96. At the time, it was being flown by LT Steven Shoemaker, and LTJG Keith Crenshaw was the RIO. This kill was scored at the same time as squadron mates LT Randy Cunningham and LTJG Willie Driscol were scoring their triple kills.

(Left Grove, right Flightleader)

51

VF-302 STALLIONS

VF-302 was the third Pacific Reserve squadron (counting VF-22L1 covered on page 12), and like VF-301, the Stallions were based at NAS Miramar. This colorfully marked F-4B was the squadron's CAG aircraft in early 1974.   (Flightleader Collection)

VF-302 added bi-centennial markings to its CAG aircraft as illustrated on F-4N, 150443. The photograph was taken on 27 March, 1976.   (Lock)

The standard squadron colors were painted on F-4N, 152970, which was photographed during a visit to Dobbins AFB, Georgia, in November 1975.   (Flightleader)

In 1978, F-4N, 153027, was the squadron's CAG aircraft. Notice the multi-colored stars painted on the fuselage along with **COMMANDER CARRIER AIR WING THIRTY**. By the time this photograph was taken, VF-302 had changed to the overall gray paint scheme. The opposite side of this aircraft is illustrated on page 3. *(Logan)*

By late 1981, the amount of color on the Stallions' CAG aircraft had been greatly reduced. All that remains on this overall gray Phantom is the yellow chevron which is edged in dark gray. Also note that VF-302 had transitioned to the F-4S by the time this photograph was taken. The aircraft is carrying live Mk 82 Snakeye bombs. The double yellow stripes on the bombs indicate that they are covered with a flame retardant material. *(Grove)*

Like its sister squadron, VF-302 also used the graded gray camouflage schemes in the early 1980s. By comparing the photographs on this page with those on page 51, it becomes evident that the four different shades of gray were painted in different places on the aircraft. Also note that patterns of the schemes also vary. Basically, there are two patterns, one being a mirror image of the other. Within these two patterns, the four shades of gray were used in various places. *(Kaston)*

Another variation of the graded gray camouflage scheme is seen on F-4S, 153851. This photograph was taken in May 1983. *(Grove)*

*At left is an overall view of F-4S, 153882, in one of the gray camouflage schemes. At right is a close-up of the **ND** tail code which was painted in light gray and edged in yellow.* *(Both Grove)*

VX-4 EVALUATORS

VX-4 was based at NAS Point Mugu, California. This unit was charged with evaluating aircraft weapon systems and developing tactics for using those weapons. This early F4H-1 was assigned to the "Evaluators" and had the squadron's dark blue band painted across the tail. The band contained four white stars and was edged in red.
(Military Aircraft Photographs)

VX-4 had acquired F-4Js when this photograph of 158350 was taken on 9 November, 1972. Note that the squadron's colorful bands have been added to the wing tips. Flashes of the same red, white, and blue colors are painted on the spine. (Bergagnini)

This Phantom was painted in the overall gray scheme and had a small black Playboy Bunny on the rudder. Note that this aircraft does not have the unit's band on the wing tips.
(Grove)

F-4J, 158360, was painted in overall gray with black markings when this photograph was taken in December 1979. The blue band does not appear anywhere on this particular aircraft.   (Flightleader)

A two-tone blue scheme was tested on F-4J, 155895. This was one of several camouflage patterns that was evaluated by VX-4 in the early 1970s. Several different types of aircraft other than Phantoms were also used in this evaluation.

(Roth)

The right side of 155895 is shown in this photograph which further illustrates this particular camouflage pattern and markings. The underside of the aircraft appears to be a flat off-white color.   (Roth)

Two of the most popular paint schemes used by VX-4 are the two illustrated on this page. One was gloss black, while the other was white. Both had large Playboy bunny logos painted on their vertical tails. Bandi 01, which was F-4J, 155539, was only one of the Phantoms to display the gloss black scheme. It is shown here as it appeared in October 1982. This Phantom was later converted to an F-4S. (Kaston)

F-4S, 158358, also wore the black Playboy bunny scheme in October 1987. (Kaston)

Above and left: A white paint scheme was used by VX-4 for only a short period of time, and it was only applied to F-4J, 158350. It is shown here as it appeared at NAS Pt. Mugu, California, in May 1977. The squadron's markings and the Playboy bunny were painted in gray. Note that this aircraft lacks all of the usual national insignias. (Flightleader)

Also very popular was this elaborate bi-centennial scheme used by VX-4. This in-flight photo shows the scheme as it was applied to the undersides of the aircraft. These markings are further illustrated on page 5.
(Picciani Aircraft Slides)

The right side of F-4J, 153088, is shown in this photograph which was taken in September 1976. Note that this aircraft has the fairing under the radome. This is unusual for an F-4J.
(Roth)

VX-4 also used the tactical paint scheme as evidenced by this photograph of F-4S, 154786. The photo is dated 28 October, 1989. *(Chong)*

F-4S, 155565, illustrates another low-visibility gray scheme used by the Evaluators. All markings were painted in the darker shade of the two-tone gray scheme. (Grove)

VX-5 VAMPIRES

The Vampires of VX-5 also used Phantoms for a short time in the 1960s. This squadron developed tactics for the delivery of air-to-ground ordnance, and they more commonly operated attack aircraft like the A-4, A-6, and A-7. The squadron's dark green tail band was edged with white, and the XE tail codes were painted white.
(Picciani Aircraft Slides)

NAVAL MISSILE CENTER

F-4J, 153074, was one of several Phantoms assigned to the Naval Missile Center (NMC) at NAS Point Mugu, California. In May 1972, this Phantom was being used as the Sparrow III test aircraft, and it had special tail markings to indicate its participation in this program. (LaBouy)

*This F-4B displays the standard scheme and markings used on Naval Missile Center aircraft in the 1970s. Notice the center's emblem on the tail and the red **NMC** on the travel pod.* (Picciani Aircraft Slides)

QF-4B, 149409, was painted over-all red-orange with standard NMC markings.
(Military Aircraft Photographs)

PACIFIC MISSILE TEST CENTER

The Pacific Missile Test Center (PMTC) replaced the Naval Missile Center and assumed its functions at NAS Point Mugu, California. One of the center's F-4Ns, 151504, is shown here as it appeared on 23 October, 1983. The aircraft was painted overall gloss gull gray. *(Kaston)*

NF-4J, 151496, had standard PMTC markings when it was photographed in March 1988. *(White)*

QF-4B, 148386, was painted in the high-visibility gloss red-orange scheme which was common to many Navy drone aircraft. Standard PMTC markings are visible on the tail. This photograph was taken at NAS North Island, California, in November 1976.

(Lock)

This close-up of the nose of 148386 provides a good look at the name **GREAT PUMPKIN** painted in white and **CHIP'S GO-KART** in black.

(Knowles)

QF-4N, 153914, illustrates the later markings used by PMTC. This aircraft was photographed while on display in October 1990.

(Kaston)

NAVAL WEAPONS EVALUATION FACILITY

The Naval Weapons Evaluation Facility (NWEF) was located at Kirtland AFB, New Mexico. One of their QF-4Bs, 149428, trails its parabrake while landing at NAF Warminister, Pennsylvania, where the drone conversions were carried out. Notice the facility's white thunderbird logo on the tail.

(Picciani Aircraft Slides)

PARACHUTE TEST CENTER

YF-4J, 151473, was assigned to the Naval Parachute Test Center at NAF El Centro, California. The white Phantom was rigged for ejection seat testing.

(Logan)

This photograph provides a look at the markings on the left side of 151473. *(Flightleader)*

NAVAL WEAPONS CENTER

The same white Phantom shown on page 63 was later assigned to the Naval Weapons Center (NWC) at NAS China Lake, California. It shows the ejection seat rail extended after a test firing. The effects of the blast from the seat's rocket motors are clearly visible. (Kaston)

This early F-4B, 148371, was assigned to the Naval Weapons Center at China Lake and carries the air station's name on its tail in black. (Flightleader Collection)

QF-4N, 150993, was also assigned to the Naval Weapons Center. Note the stylized eagle on the tail. It is holding lightning bolts, missiles, and an anchor in its talons. The famous Phantom "spook" is painted on the splitter plate. (Flightleader Collection)